Itty-Bitty Teeny-Tiny

Word Books

20 Little Books That Give Kids Practice With 300 Key Words—and Build Early Reading Skills

by Kama Einhorn

My Classroom Words

My Little Book of Pond Words

My BUGGY Book

SCHOLASTIC
PROFESSIONAL BOOKS

New York • Toronto • London • Auckland • Sydney • Mexico City
New Delhi • Hong Kong • Buenos Aires

For Nick Macri,
my fairy godfather.

Cover design by **Maria Lilja**

Interior design by **Holly Grundon**

Art research by **Denise Ortiz**

ISBN: 0-439-41127-0

Copyright © 2003 by Scholastic Inc.

Printed in the U.S.A.

1 2 3 4 5 6 7 8 9 10   40   09 08 07 06 05 04 03

Contents

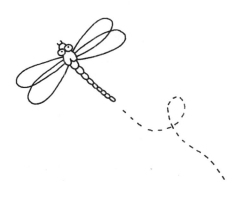

The Mini-Books

PLACES

SEASONS & WEATHER

FOOD & FUN

ANIMALS

BASIC CONCEPTS

Introduction

Welcome to **Itty-Bitty Teeny-Tiny Word Books!** *These 20 little themed picture dictionaries will help kids expand their vocabulary and build reading confidence. Adorable and easy to assemble, they'll fit right into kids' pockets, making them easy to take home and read again and again. And often, they'll fit right into your curriculum, helping children build content-area vocabulary.*

We hope your students enjoy these itty-bitty literacy builders!

Using the Mini-Books in Your Classroom

Once the mini-books have been assembled, you can enjoy them in many ways:

* ☀ Have children color the illustrations.

* ☀ Invite children to complete the sentence on the back page, when included.

* ☀ Read the book together as children follow along.

* ☀ Have children pair up and read the books to each other.

* ☀ Send the books home and have children read them to their families.

Making the Mini-Books

It's best to assemble the books together as a class (you might assemble one yourself to demonstrate first, so children can see the finished product). Each book is assembled the same way:

1. Copy the page on standard 8 1/2-inch by 11-inch paper, making a double-sided page.

2. Cut along the dashed lines; fold along the solid lines

3. Place the pages in order and staple along the spine.

Building Vocabulary
With the Mini-books

Each book is packed with content-area vocabulary, making them great for second-language learners or kids who need extra vocabulary development. Here are some ways to extend the learning. First, copy each mini-book page onto two pages, so you can cut apart the pages and use them as "word cards." With these cards, you can play a variety of games:

Flashcards: Children look at the cards and time themselves as they read them.

Concentration: Use two sets of the same set of cards to play this familiar matching game.

ABC Order: Children can put the cards in alphabetical order.

Sort & Classify: Use cards from two or three different books. Shuffle them and have children separate them into the correct pile.

Writing Prompt Cards: Put cards in a pile and have the child draw a card. They then write a sentence using that word.

I live in

_____

16

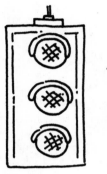

traffic
light

14

house

3

post office

12

firehouse

5

car

10

police
officer

7

school

2

school bus

15

store

4

stop sign

13

police station

6

mail carrier

11

fire fighter

8

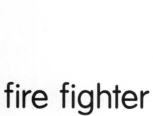

flag

9

scarecrow

16

My Little Book of

Farm Words

1

goat

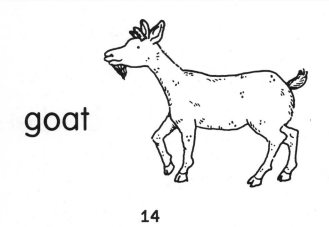

14

cow

3

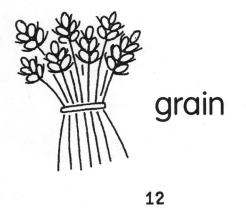

grain

12

sheep

5

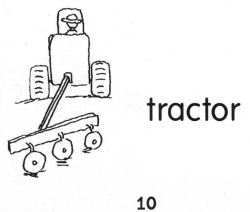

tractor

10

horse

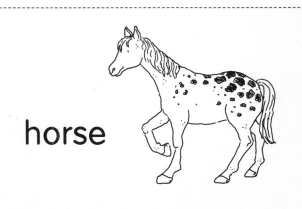

7

barn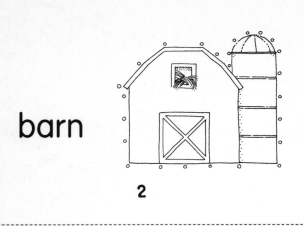

2

farmer

15

rooster

4

 chicken

13

 milk

6

egg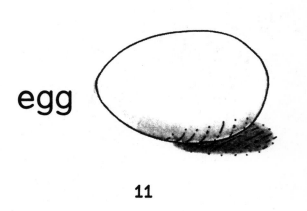

11

 duck

8

pig

9

My favorite thing at the zoo is

_____

_____

_____

16

My Miniature Zoo

1

fox

14

yak

3

porcupine

12

alligator

5

chimp

10

penguin

7

lion

2

snake

15

seal

4

elephant

13

duck

6

tiger

11

hippo

8

anteater

9

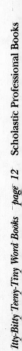

My favorite pond animal:

_____

16

My Little Book of

Pond Words

1

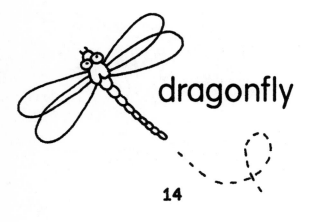

dragonfly

14

frogs

3

geese

12

lily pads

5

rock

10

bird

7

toads

2

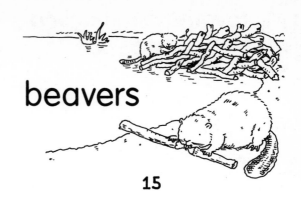

beavers

15

fish

4

cattails

13

turtle

6

snake

11

ducks

8

rabbit

9

My favorite kind of
weather is

_____

16

What's the
Weather?

1

tornado

14

wind

3

lightning

12

snow

5

umbrella

10

hail

7

sun

2

rain

4

fog

6

hot

8

snowballs!

15

blizzard

13

thermometer

11

cold

9

I made this mini-book
in the month of

_____

16

New Year

14

February

3

November

12

April

5

September

10

June

7

January

2

seasons

15

March

4

December

13

May

6

October

11

July

8

August

9

I like to celebrate

_____

16

Winter Holidays

1

family

14

Christmas tree

3

cookies

12

dreidel

5

candy cane

10

present

7

December

2

January

15

menorah

4

Chinese New Year

13

Kwanzaa candles

6

Ramadan

11

Diwali

8

Las Posadas

9

Me in my favorite outfit:

clothes

for All Seasons

1

dress

14

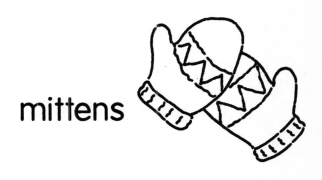

pants

3

raincoat

12

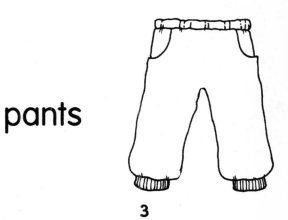

mittens

5

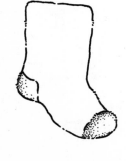

sock

10

vest

7

 shirt

2

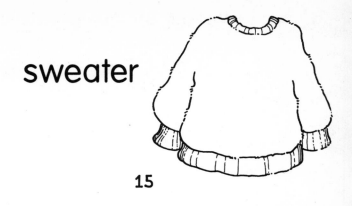 sweater

15

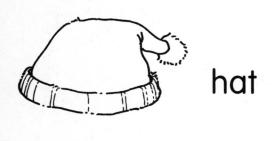 hat

4

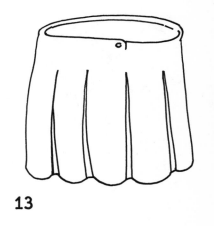 skirt

13

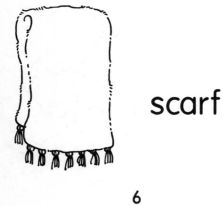 scarf

6

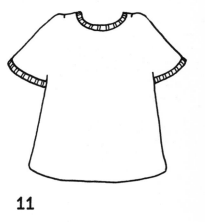 t-shirt

11

shorts

8

bathing suit

9

My favorite fruit:

_____

My favorite vegetable:

_____

16

My Tiny Book of
Fruits & Vegetables

1

corn

14

oranges

3

broccoli

12

banana

5

pears

10

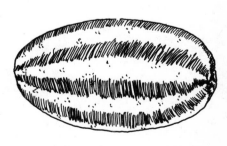

watermelon

7

apples

2

celery

15

lemons

4

peas

13

strawberries

6

carrot

11

pineapple

8

grapes

9

I would like to add

_____

to my lunchbox.

16

ITTY-BITTY

Lunchbox Book

1

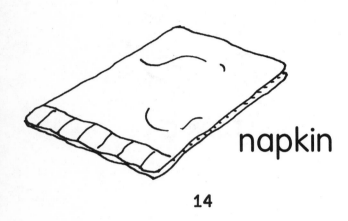

napkin

14

apple

3

 raisins

12

juice

5

 pizza

10

soup

7

sandwich

2

thermos

15

chips

4

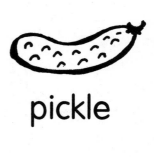

pickle

13

 milk

6

carrot

11

oranges

8

cookies

9

My favorite thing to
do at recess is:

_____

16

Playground in
Your Pocket!

1

running

14

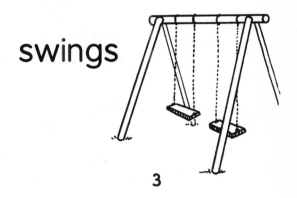

swings

3

soccer

12

jungle gym

5

hopscotch

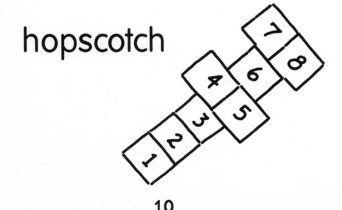

10

reading

7

This book belongs to:

_____

2

basketball

15

see-saw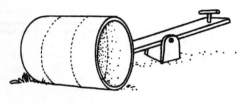

4

friends

13

slide

6

sandbox

11

softball

8

jump rope

9

My favorite way to
travel is by

_____

16

wagon

14

bus

3

truck

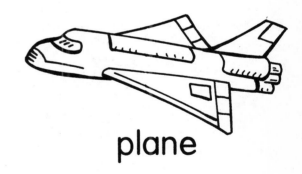

plane

12

running

10

skateboard

7

car

2

rocket

15

train

4

van

13

bike

6

scooter

11

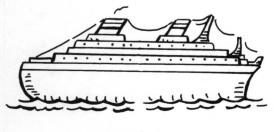

ship

8

walking

9

My favorite bug is:

_____

16

My
BUGGY
Book

1

ladybug

14

caterpillar

3

butterfly

12

bee

5

pill bug

10

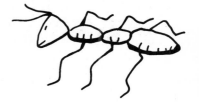

ant

7

spider

2

beetle

15

fly

4

stick bug

13

dragonfly

6

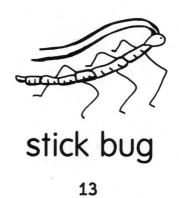

moth

11

fireflies

8

millipede

9

I would like to take
care of a baby

_____

16

gosling

14

piglet

12

lamb

10

My Book of

Baby

Animals

1

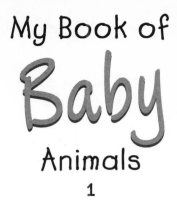

cub

3

puppy

5

calf

7

duckling

2

owlet

15

kitten

4

tadpole

13

seal pup

6

joey

11

chick

8

pony

9

My favorite big animal is:

_____

16

1

ostrich

14

polar bear

3

dinosaur

12

whale

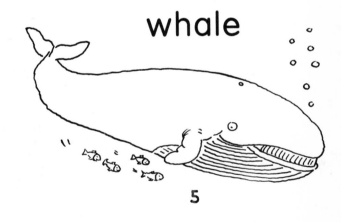

5

tiger

10

jaguar

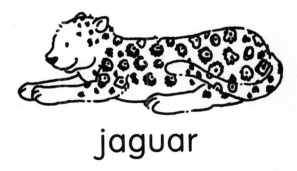

7

elephant

2

camel

15

rhinoceros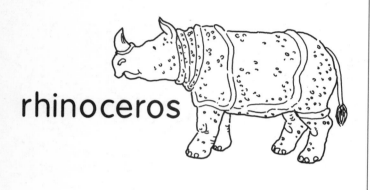

4

panda

13

horse

6

zebra

11

buffalo

8

moose

9

I would like a

_____

for a pet.

16

Pets

1

iguana

14

dog

3

snake

12

gerbil

5

parakeet

10

mouse

7

cat

2

an imaginary pet!

15

frog

4

rabbit

13

hamster

6

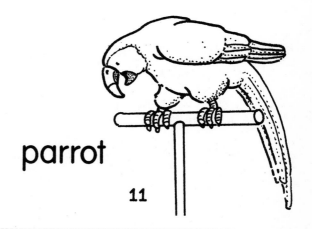

parrot

11

fish

8

turtle

9

Right now I feel

_____

16

Feelings & Faces

1

 angry

sad

14

3

silly

mad

12

5

sleepy

worried

10

7

frustrated

2

 funny
face!

15

happy

4

calm

13

content

6

nervous

11

surprised

8

excited

9

My favorite shape is

_____

16

A Small
Book
of Shapes

1

box

14

square

3

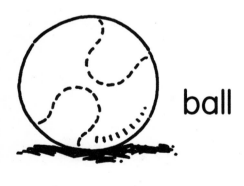
ball

12

oval

5

cube

10

octagon

7

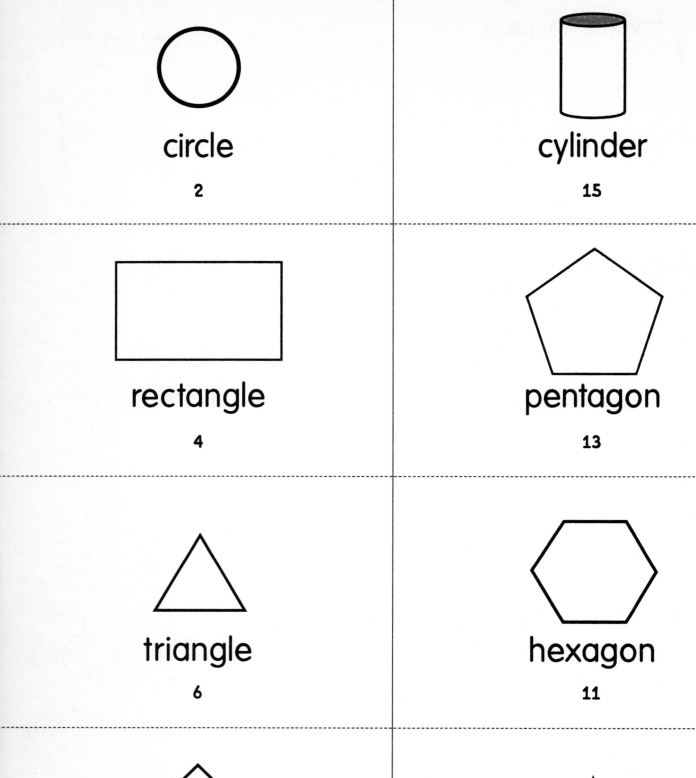

circle

2

cylinder

15

rectangle

4

pentagon

13

triangle

6

hexagon

11

diamond

8

star

9

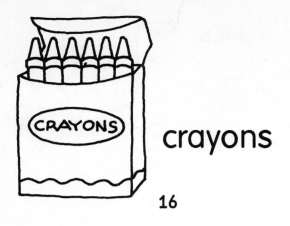

crayons

16

My Classroom Words

1

scissors

14

chair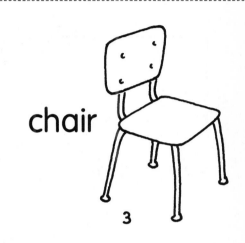

3

door

12

teacher

5

clock

10

book

7

desk

2

blocks

15

easel

4

 map

13

 student

6

 glue

11

notebook

8

pencil

9

My favorite color is:

_____

16

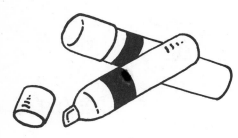

markers

14

green

3

paints

12

blue

5

black

10

brown

7

red

2

pencils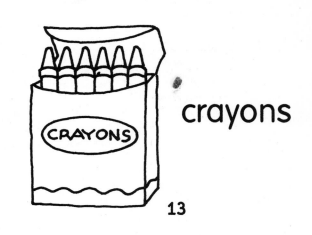

15

yellow

4

 crayons

13

orange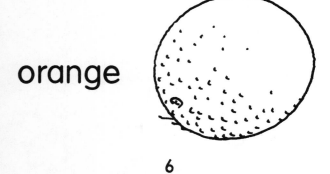

6

 rainbow

11

purple

8

pink

9

Notes

_____

_____

_____

_____

_____

_____

_____

_____

_____

_____

_____

_____

Notes